LET IT BE
Easy

Poems and Short Stories of Inspiration, Love and Nature

JESSE GOURDET

FOREWORD
BY Jessica Gourdet-Murray, MPH
Cover design by Jason Bremer

NEW YORK

Praises for *Let it be Easy*:

Enchanting phrases and skillfully crafted verses makes these poems a melody of rhythm and imagery.
> —**The International Library of Poetry**

The depth of feelings and human insights expressed in *Let It Be Easy* captured me.
> —**Arthur W. Murray**

I have enjoyed looking over your poetry and I love the story of the Goddess of the Waterfall. The poetry is fresh, straightforward and honest.
> —**Susan Kendrick**

Let it be Easy shows that we must take time to enjoy certain things in life.
> —**Josephine Genna, Nevada**

What I like about this book is that it has a little bit of everything for everyone, young or old.
> —**Fenol Jean, Maryland**

These beautiful and timeless verses evoke true love that transcends time and space. Jesse's poems have passion and fire in them.
> —**Iris Davis, New York**

Like a first-class French meal, each poem is catered to individual taste, executed to perfection with heart and passion.
— Greg Gourdet, Oregon

Soul Searching and entertaining. ***Let it be Easy*** is a must for your collection.
—Antoinette Graham, New York

Your poems are really great. I felt your heart as each spoke to me.
—Joyce Belle Edelbrock

Jesse's new book is elegant – fresh air for the soul. We should dip into each day.
—Jerry Berkson, Great Neck, NY

What a great book! "Let It Be Easy" should be read by everyone. It is very uplifting and positive. My favorites are "True Wisdom" and "A Smile".
—**Tipton Golias, Founder and Chairman of Helena Laboratories, Texas**

"Let It Be Easy" is very soothing. It speaks to my heart and removes my day to day stress.
—**Donna J. Fitzmartin, VP Ancillary Services and Case Management, New York Community Hospital**

"Happiness was born a twin."
—Lord Byron
Share *Let it be Easy* with a friend.

Copyright © 2010 by Jesse Gourdet
All rights reserved in all countries
Printed in the USA

ISBN 10: 0979812445
ISBN 13: 9780979812446
LCCN: 2010910456

For information:
Jesse Gourdet
241-88A Oak Park Drive
Douglaston, NY 11362
Phone: 718-428-9729

E-mail: *Jgourdet@aol.com*

To my wife and my muse
Yanick

Here is my secret. It is very simple:
it is with the heart that one sees well.
What is essential is invisible to the eye.
—*Antoine de Saint Exupéry*

CONTENTS

ACKNOWLEDGMENTS xv
FOREWORD xix
INTRODUCTION xxi

PART ONE: Spiritual Growth

DIALING GOD. 4
LET IT BE EASY 5
A BRIGHTER WORLD 6
CAUGHT IN THE THICKET 7
THE GIFT. 8
WHAT IF. 9
A MAGIC THOUGHT 10
THE POWER OF FORGIVENESS. 11
THE LONG JOURNEY 12
PRESENT MOMENT 13
THE SECRET 14
TULIP 15
CHASING CLOUDS. 16
THE POINT OF LIFE 17
FREE 18
DANCING IN THE PARK. 19
THE LIGHT 21
PEACE AND TRANQUILITY 22
A LITTLE PLACE IN THE SUN 23
GONE WITH THE WIND 24
BREAKFAST AT BRUCE'S BAKERY. 25

FIRST STEP	26
NOLAN	27
THANKS	28
VICTORY	29
THE HEART OF THE LOTUS	30
RESPONSIBILITY	31
ONE MORE TIME	32
TRUE WISDOM	33

PART TWO: Love

FIRST LOVE	36
I WISH	37
NICKIE	38
UNCONDITIONAL LOVE	39
YOU AND I	40
EMBRACING THE DIVINE	41
THE SPACE BETWEEN US	42
A CRY IN THE NIGHT	43
WHEN I AM WITH YOU	44
CHRYSALIS	45
THE LONELY BUTTERFLY	46
SPECTRUM OF BEAUTY	47
SALSA DANCERS	48
RUSSIAN KISSES	49
DAUGHTER OF HEAVEN	50
A WHISPER IN THE WIND	52
A GLIMPSE OF YOU	53
THE LOST FLOWER	54
WOUNDS OF ILLUSION	55
THE LADY OF THE GARDEN	57

THE PURSUIT OF HAPPINESS 58
BOUNDLESS ABYSS 59
THE LADY OF JAMAICA ESTATES 60
HAND IN HAND 61
MATILDA 62
A NEW YORK MINUTE. 64
LOVE ON-LINE 65

PART THREE: Nature

AUTUMN'S LEAVES 68
POWDERHOUSE IN THE MORNING 70
NOXONTOWN 71
BIRD'S NEST 72
A MORNING CONCERT 73
A BIRD'S SONG 74
GOOD-BYE 75
CENTRAL PARK 76
A SMILE 77
THE HOMELESS LADY. 78
THE CHILDREN OF DR. GRANT 79
THE EVENING STAR 80
BOAT PEOPLE 81
DREAMING IN THE SUN 82
I WILL SURVIVE 83
A BRIGHT MORNING STAR 84

PART FOUR: SHORT STORIES

THE GODDESS OF THE WATERFALL 88
DR. HUM LITTLE KITTY 94
GREG'S GOLDFISH 97

THE KING'S GOLDFISH 99
THE RABBI'S GIFT 102

ALPHABETIZED INDEX 106

ABOUT THE AUTHOR 109

ACKNOWLEDGMENTS

In his poem "A Minor Bird", the poet Robert Frost wrote: "There must be something wrong, in wanting to silence any song." These verses have been a guiding light for me in my writing.

I wish to acknowledge the inspiration I received from best-selling author and lecturer Brian Tracy. A few years ago, I mailed him one of my poems. He sent me a copy of the poem "Don't Quit". This gesture was an eye opener. The poem "Don't Quit" provided me with the persistence needed to make this book a reality.

Here is the poem:

Don't Quit

When things are wrong as they sometimes will.
When the road you're trudging seems all up hill.
When funds are low and the debts are high.
And you want to smile, but you have to sigh.
When care is pressing you down a bit.
Rest, if you must, but don't you quit.
Life is queer with its twists and turns.
As every one of us sometimes learns.
And many a failure turns about
When he might have won had he stuck it out:

Don't give up though the pace seems slow
You may succeed with another blow.
Success is failure turned inside out
The silver tint of the clouds of doubt.
And you never can tell how close you are.
It may be near when it seems so far:
So stick to the fight when you're hardest hit
It's when things seem worst that you must not Quit.
—Author Unknown

I am particularly grateful to my daughter Jessica, who helped me all along the way, from reading the poems to the preparation of the manuscript for publication. Her insights helped to shape the book. Her dedication is well appreciated.

I am grateful to Ruby Cooper who gave me so much encouragement at the beginning of my writing.

I am especially grateful to my past and present associates, the healthcare professionals with whom I have shared theses poems and stories. Many listened to or read the poems. Some people gave me inspiration or encouragement; others helped me to rewrite the poems and stories, sometimes changing them in both language and contents. For your inspiration and input into this book I would like to present my heartfelt thanks to all of you.

Special thank to my brother Gustave Edouard and to my network members Joseph and Andie Gedeon, Manasse Decady, Rollin Zephyrin, Michel Bazile, M.D., Michel Coulanges, LL.L, Marie-Ange Coulanges, LL.L.

My deepest gratitude to my friends and fellow Rotarians of the Gold Coast-Lake Success Club for their unwavering support and encouragement. Thanks to Diana Toma and Alain Beauvais for their contribution to the book.

FOREWORD

By
Jessica Gourdet-Murray, MPH

Love, nature and inspiration
That's the promise of ***Let it be Easy*** and it delivers. Some of the poems helped me go through difficult moments. Others brought a smile on my face. Most of all, this book had a great influence on me as it got me closer to my father. I was his sounding board, the first person to read and critique these poems.

People who have read this book have found it quite inspiring and entertaining.

I hope you enjoy it.

Buy a copy of ***Let it be Easy*** for a friend.

INTRODUCTION

Most of us have our favorite story. For me, it's the story of the wise lady and the young man.
That story touched me the first time I heard it and it has stayed with me ever since.

Here it is:
In a small village lived a wise lady. The people of the village go to her with their problems, and she helps them.
One young man, however, wanted to outwit the wise lady. He decided he would go to her with a bird clasped in his hands. He would ask the wise lady if the bird was dead or alive. If the wise lady says the bird was dead, he would open his hands and let the bird fly. If the wise lady says the bird was alive, he would crush the bird with his hands and drop its lifeless body on the ground, thereby destroying the reputation of the wise lady.
On the day of the open market, the young man went to the wise lady and addressed her in front of a large crowd.
"Wise lady, O wise lady, what do I have in my hands?" he asked.
"You have a bird in your hand," replied the wise lady.
"Is this bird dead or is this bird alive?" continued the young man. The wise lady looked at him firmly in the eyes and said:
"The bird is in your hand, my friend."

That's the story I was told.

And so it is with all of us. We can complain:"life sucks," or we can *"let it be easy."* The choice is ours. I have chosen the latter path and this is what I'd like to share with you in these poems and short stories.

Jesse Gourdet,
Douglaston, NY
May 20, 2010

PART ONE:
Spiritual Growth

Dialing God

I was dreading the outcome
I felt afraid of what's to come.
My heart was pounding,
My body was shaking.
What's going to happen?
Was it the end?
My mind was set on doom and gloom.
Am I heading straight to the tomb?
I closed my eyes and made a call
To God who is always there for us all.
I felt a hand touching my hand.
"Let it be" was the command.
Then I heard a voice singing this song
That has the power to make us strong:
"We shall overcome!"
"We shall overcome!"
A sense of peace overtook me.
"Just let it be, God is with me"
Whatever the outcome, it's fine.
"Thy will be done, not mine."

Let It Be Easy

How hard is it for an acorn to grow into an oak tree?
How hard is it for the smallest creatures to be free?
Easy does it; God said, "Let it be easy."

How hard is it for a whale to take off from the ocean floors?
How hard is it for a sea wave to crash against the shores?
Easy does it; God said, "Let it be easy."

How hard is it for a cocoon to transform into a butterfly?
How hard is it for an ant to stock its winter supply?
Easy does it. God said, "Let it be easy."

How hard is it for a star to light up the darkest night?
How hard is it for spring season to return for our delight?
Easy does it. God said, "Let it be easy."

When you are facing insurmountable difficulties,
Remember God is providing you with opportunities.
Easy does it, God said, "Let it be easy."

A Brighter World

Once upon a time there was a little girl whose name was Kris.
Her mother departed without even giving her a good-bye kiss.
Her grandmother raised her with much love and compassion.
Over the years Kris lived a really boring life with no passion.

She often asked herself why her life didn't have more significance.
At night, she would get on her knees to pray for spiritual guidance.
Dismissing the saying: "Most people die with their song still unplayed,"
She believed that her wishes were not denied by God but only delayed.

One day, she went on a field trip on the site of an old volcanic eruption.
She found a rare stone, the size of an egg, which filled her with emotion.
She took the stone to the nearest brook and washed it really clean.
It turned out to be the most beautiful stone she had ever seen.

She polished the stone to a brilliant shine and inserted it in her heart.
She became totally enlightened as if her life had received a jumpstart.
She shared the light with others, even helping old flames to rekindle.
It was like holding a candle for other people to light their own candle.

Where ever Kris went she sowed the seed of love in the light.
She helped the multitude to be relieved of their plight.
In return for her kindness they made her life a little sweeter.
Some people say: *"She made the world a little brighter."*

Caught in the Thicket

Abraham's great relationship with God had set him apart.
God's request to seal their love tested his father's heart.
Still, when asked for the ultimate sacrifice,
He didn't hesitate to pay the high price.

He followed the course to sacrifice his son,
But God only wanted to teach him a lesson.
The blood of a ram ensured Abraham's redemption.
And God blessed his descendants with a mighty nation.

Three thousand years later under a similar condition,
Out of love, God gave his only son for our salvation.
The blood of the Lamb of God was shed explicitly,
"That they might have life and have it more abundantly."

Five thousand years later we are back in falsehood,
We have lost the power of love and of brotherhood.
Life is a special and beautiful gift to enjoy.
God is the true source of our hope and joy.

References: Genesis: 22:1-12
John: 10:10

The Gift

Every day when I wake up
I bow my head in gratitude,
For it seems like yesterday
When I thought I was forgotten.
And then I received the gift,
That made all the difference in my life.
With you came the happiness I searched for,
For such a long time.
In my most difficult moments,
I know I can turn to you,
For comfort and advice
Only a friend can give.
Now that I hold you in my arms,
I don't want to let you go.
You are my priceless gift
And I am yours forever.

What if...

What if I was living my perfect life?
Going my way, doing my thing.
Helping others to reach for the stars.
And all the while being certain
That my spaceship
Was under God's command.
What if...

A Magic Thought

Now I feel your pain and your sorrow,
Will there ever be a brighter tomorrow?
A magic thought in seven words,
Mightier than the mightiest swords,
Has the power to open heaven.
Yes, the words count is seven,
They are hidden deep in your heart,
Pluck them out for a fresh start.
It's a new day
When you can say,
Very loud and clear
For the universe to hear,
I am sorry and I love you!
I am sorry and I love you!

The Power of Forgiveness

Trapped between you and your ultimate happiness
Are solid blocks that obscure your consciousness.
They are called anger and fear, greed and apathy.
You can't move in high gear without empathy.

These blocks can be released if you learn to forgive.
This takes more courage than you may want to give.
By forgiving yourself and your fellow human being,
You are bound to create a life that is truly inspiring.

The Long Journey
To Josey Allayna Cruz

You gave vision to the tiny acorn
To grow into a mighty oak tree.
You gave courage to the whale
To master the great oceans.

You gave power to the lion
To rule over the wild kingdom.
You gave boldness to the eagle
To dare to face the rising sun.

You gave beauty to the flowers
To bring joy and love to all.
Why not inspire me to blossom fully
In my long journey towards the stars?

Present Moment

There is a place within your heart,
Where the future is bold and bright.
Once you see it you will know,
It provides inspiration to grow.

Open your heart to enchantment
And dwell in the present moment,
To sow the seeds of things to come,
Of all that you can become.

Get off your ass and do what it takes,
You can still erase your mistakes.
Seize the moment; it's not too late
To start over with a clean slate.

You can build a monument to last,
No matter what you did in the past.
And in the midst of inner beauty
May you find peace and serenity.

The Secret

Look into yourself to discover who you really are,
The highest expression of God created thus far.
This is a secret that has been hidden from mankind,
Revealed only to initiates with great power of mind.

The spiritual and secular leaders over the centuries
Have kept this secret hidden in complex mysteries
And when it was revealed, it was only partial;
The modus operandi was concealed in a ritual.

The people who use the secret are sworn "not to tell".
Their creative process raised them to a higher level.
They know where they're going and they often get there,
Once they master their fears and gain the power to dare.

You can make your life wonderful
And get up every day cheerful
Unleash your God-given power bit by bit
Listen to your soul and above all don't quit.

Tulip

Tulip is a cute little dog raised in a well to do family.
She is cared for with a lot of love, she is very friendly.
She takes her morning stroll with the rising of the sun.
She goes running in the park and has a lot of fun.

Never in her life has she missed a hearty meal.
Professional grooming enhances her sex appeal.
Her appointment with the vet is done on a regular schedule.
Tulip is as happy as a dog can be without breaking any rule.

But some dogs are destined to nothing but bad luck.
They are abandoned and sometimes they get struck.
Wherever they turn they get the short end of the stick.
Those who don't like dogs greet them with a kick.

Are those dogs the victims of their genetic pool?
Would they be better off with skin covered with wool?
A dog cannot do much about its precarious condition.
We human can, we are on a journey of transformation.

Chasing Clouds

We spend our lives chasing clouds in the sky,
Oblivious to the fact that they will always come by.

We fight unceasingly against our situations,
Not realizing that they're there to teach us lessons.

When we learn to pierce the clouds by soaring,
We'll find that the light was always shining.

We will reach that level of transformation
Where a problem generates its own solution.

When your sky is dark and cloudy,
Take this little advice it will come in handy:

Raise your inner self higher with no fear.
On God's level the sky is always clear.

The Point of Life

Do you ask, "What's the purpose of my existence?"
Ask no more. The answer is buried in your essence.
Your life was given to you to make it shine in the light,
To benefit you and humanity without having to fight.

The people and circumstances that come into your life
Are there for a reason, to help you navigate the strife,
Like a beacon in the night they help you see the rocks,
Easing the rough edges of the school of hard knocks.

We go through many lives to purify our souls.
We still fail even after reading all the scrolls.
Only a few are born-giants like the mythical Cyclops.
Our awareness increases as the mind slowly develops.

Be good to yourself and ensure your well-being.
It is a blessing to get up in the morning,
To breathe the fresh air, to love and to be loved,
To be of service and to get problems solved.

Free
To Crissy

I want to be free,
Free to fly away
Like a butterfly.

I see, the sun is shining,
The sky is mine for flying.

I want to be free,
Free to fly away
Like a butterfly.

God gave me wings for flying,
No clouds to stop my climbing.

I want to be free,
Free to fly away
Like a butterfly.

Dancing In The Park
To the seniors of Stuyvesant Park

Summer heat fell on the condo,
Friends are waiting; let's go.
We'll have a nice gathering
And do some serious dancing.

We have a willing teacher,
She'll bring a C D player.
It's such a beautiful day.
Oldies and goodies we play.

Dancing in the park in daytime,
What a way to have a good time.
It brings back the youth
That eludes us, in truth.

In unison we clap our hands.
The sound resonates in the land.
Our feet are up in the air
As we breathe the fresh air.

Up on the branches of a tree,
Birds are watching with glee.
We try the new dance in stride,
It's called the Electric Slide.

It's like "Dance at Bougival,"
Renoir does have a rival,
Who captures the scene before dark
Of seniors dancing in the park.

The Light

There is a light in the universe
That shines over darkness.
Once you become one with the light,
You will never see darkness again.

Peace and Tranquility

Don't be so naïve
As to think you can change the world.
Learn to be and then to do.

Don't be upset
When you can't find what you seek.
Peace and tranquility reside inside of you.

Don't be sad
Rejoice and be grateful for what you have,
Time is shorter than you think.

A Little Place in the Sun

The time has come to serve your world,
May God grant you a little place in the sun!
With good habits you can reach great heights,
With bad habits you are doomed for the pit.

The good news is that there is a key.
Deep inside of you is a little spark,
Hidden like a needle in a haystack,
Ready to show you the way.

Make it bright like a shining light.
See it and feel comfortable with it,
And like a beacon in the darkness,
It will illuminate your life.

With clear vision you can see the road ahead.
Follow the path in the direction of your dreams,
Braving the shadows that lurk along the way.
May God grant you a little place in the sun!

Gone With the Wind

I have often wondered what ever happened
To the great men and women of yesteryear.

Men and women who stuck to their beliefs
Until their dreams came true.

Men and women who faced the wrath of the seas
In search of new worlds and meaningful lives.

Men and women with passionate love
Who gave themselves to each other eternally.

And still I ask the questions:
Where had they gone?

The great men and women of yesteryear,
Gone with the wind?

Breakfast at Bruce's Bakery
To my GCLS friends

Happy people have breakfast at Bruce's,
Unhappy people go to other places.
Happy people are courteous and kind,
Unhappy people couldn't care less about mankind.

Happy people improve less fortunate people's situation,
Unhappy people are resigned to their condition.
Happy people follow in Nike's footsteps and just do it,
Unhappy people procrastinate and cannot get out of it.

Happy people do first thing first to fulfill their desires,
Unhappy people are busy putting out imaginary fires.
Happy people stick like a stamp until delivery is made,
Unhappy people give up easily or keep changing trade.

Happy people believe that to do is to be and to be is to do,
Unhappy people are lost in the "do be do be do."
Happy people have breakfast at Bruce's,
Unhappy people go to other places.

First Step

    The goal was clear
    and seems so near.
    The cause was worthy
    and the hurdles many.

"Take the first step," the old man said,
"and the rest will take care of itself."
But, in spite of my good intention,
the day went by with no action.

I paused for self-examination in the night.
I then realized that the old man was right.
If only I had taken the first step as told,
    I wouldn't be left out in the cold.

Nolan

Now that you are anointed
You can conquer the horizon.
Show discipline and determination,
Infinite wisdom will be with you.

Thanks

I wake up in the morning light,
Blessed with grace and delight.
As I face towards the sun above me,
I leave the shadows behind me.

I welcome this time to accomplish my task,
Knowing that life will give me what I ask.
With joy and gratitude I accept my blessings,
Flowing like a river in pleasant surroundings.

I give thanks for the wonderful environment
God created for my maximum achievement.
I find peace and happiness all along my way.
I love and appreciate what I have every day.

Victory

The day will come,
I'll be a winner,
I can see it,
I can feel it.

The day will come,
When I'll say, "I did it"
I can see it
I can feel it.

The message is clear,
I must follow the road
That leads to victory
And to the sun that warms the heart.

The day will come,
I'll be a winner,
I can see it,
I can feel it.

The Heart of the Lotus

"Follow the hero's path
from your abyss
and you will be lifted
to eternal bliss"

Have no fear, I lead the way.
Keep inner calm amid turbulence.
In the heart of the lotus flower.
I find peace.

Responsibility

This past Friday, I heard the story of Peter.
He was having dinner with Jesus and the disciples,
When he made a promise he couldn't keep.

"Lord," said Peter, "I am ready to die with you".
Jesus answered: "Peter, before the cock crows twice,
You will deny me three times."

That night at the trial
Peter denied knowing Jesus three times,
In order to save his own skin.

By the third denial, the cock had crowed twice.
He remembered the master's words.
"He broke down and wept."

That was his moment of truth.
He became responsible
And Jesus gave him the key to heaven.

One More Time

You try to do your best,
And still, you are pursuing your quest.
At day's end, you leave the work place
With a tired look on your face.

You walk slowly down the hall,
Sliding your hand over the wall,
Your shoulder is bent, your head is down.
Deep in thought, as you go down.

You tried everything,
Nothing goes in full swing.
You want to throw in the towel,
Before the sound of the bell.

That's when you should know,
That good is not good enough,
Excellence can only take you so far,
Especially, if you've come from afar.

But in the end, what really counts
Is to do whatever it takes, by all accounts.
You cannot reach the sublime,
Unless you try one more time.

True Wisdom

You do the best you can,
Yet life throws curveballs at you.

You make preparation,
Yet, the worst that could happen happens.

If Murphy's Law is for the other guy,
Why am I am hit so hard in the face?

Don't let negative thoughts
Rob you of the good to come.

Follow your cat and take a little nap.
Inspiration comes in quiet moments.

It is ok to live with hopes and dreams.
Failures are but lessons that teach us how to win.

PART TWO:
Love

First Love

It was the age of innocence,
We longed for unveiling our essence.
We fell in love with each other,
Upon meeting one another.

I laid my forehead over yours and then
I discovered a taste of heaven,
Like a monk in meditation,
Lost in God's contemplation.

There was magic in the moment.
We became one with the environment.
Losing all sense of space and time,
As we created a new paradigm.

I Wish

I wish I had someone,
Someone to cherish me in the morning
And to hold me tight in the evening.

I wish I had someone,
Someone to cheer me up when I am sad
And to make me laugh until I am glad.

I wish I had someone,
Someone to console me, to be friendly
And to be with me when I am lonely.

I wish I had someone,
Someone to share my joy and happiness
And to feel my pain and emptiness.

I wish I had someone,
Someone to cut me flowers in springtime
And to give me kisses all the time.

I wish I had someone,
Someone to love with all my heart
And that someone is you, my sweetheart.

Nickie

We've been friends
For so many years,
But tonight
In this coffee bar,
Over a café latte
I look in your eyes,
And suddenly
I realize
That I love you.

Unconditional Love

My heart is open to you.
I love you, for who you are,
With unconditional love
That will last for eternity.

You and I

You and I are so different
Yet we are so inseparable.

This symbiotic relationship
Follows the laws of nature,

Where two completely opposite bodies
Attract each other in close union.

You are a dynamic ball of fire;
I am a lake on a windless day.

You are on a race with time,
I move slowly like a turtle.

You are a goal-striving mechanism;
I like to stop and smell the flowers.

You are so attractive;
I succumb to your charm.

You care for me;
I care for you.

That's why we are so together
Even though we are a world apart.

Embracing the Divine

When I hold you in my arms
I am embracing the divine.
Sensing the softness of your skin
Dissolves my tense feeling.

The energy is flowing,
Thanks to this sweet grounding.
I feel connected to you
With a love that is true.

The Space between Us

There is a space between us
That only love can fill.
I give to you my heart,
I ask for yours in return.

Love is a powerful magnet
That draws two hearts together.
Let this magnetic force
Fill the space between us.

A Cry in the Night

Love is a cry in the night
That cuts through the silence.
The cry of a baby
Yearning for affection.

When I Am With You

When I am with you
Life takes on a new dimension.
Where there is a circle I see a sphere,
Where there is a square I see a cube.
Where there is a triangle I see a pyramid.

I put on my 3-D glasses,
I see the whole universe in your eyes.
My love for you grows exponentially.
I fall in love
When I am with you.

Chrysalis

I was wandering aimlessly one day,
Having nothing to do, going no special way,
When in the distance my eyes fell upon you.
Divine apparition! Was I dreaming or was it true?

Dressed for love in a light emerald gown,
On her erected head rested a golden crown.
I fell under the charm of this celestial radiance.
I consulted a seer to ask for spiritual guidance.

By the new moon, she said, your monarchical face
Shall be revealed to me in a warm and sacred place.
I exuded joy and great expectation.
Having you is having the universe without limitation.

But the months have passed year after year
And to my dismay, you're still not free and clear.
Like the Psalmist I cry, "How long will thou forget me?
How long wilt thou hide thy face away from me?"

O beautiful lady! The best of time has come
To purify your soul and say to life: Welcome!
When the chrysalis kisses its cocoon good-bye,
It's just the beginning of life for a new butterfly.

The Lonely Butterfly

It was a clear and pleasant evening.
The wind was blowing a gentle breeze,
The air was nippy and soothing.
We were in communion with the environment.

In the distance we could hear reggae music
Mixed with the song of a cheerful bird,
The passionate notes of a flute player
And the persistent sound of a grasshopper.

It was then that it came along,
In its monarchical splendor,
Stopping from flower to flower,
Sipping the nectar of immortality.

Messenger from another world,
Did you bring good news
Or was it bad?
Please tell us, we want to know now.

The lonely butterfly continued its flight
And inebriated on the drink of the gods,
It drew the outline of the sign of love in the air
And then disappeared to enjoy more flowers.

Spectrum of Beauty

She was like a shining light
With a reflection on my soul,
Shading a spectrum of beauty
With the colors of the rainbow.

As I bathed in her radiance
The brightness and beauty of our love
Was captured as a hologram
To shine in 3-D, undivided and whole.

Salsa Dancers

They glow over the dancing floor in their Open Shines.
The luscious twist of their hips enhances the Susie Q's.
Their hands move gracefully in the Cuban Step.

Keep your eyes open for the Mambo Jazz.
Their bodies turn flawlessly in the Cross Body Lead.
Their beautiful smile enlightens the Embrace Turn.

You can taste the flavor of Celia Cruz,
Admire the style of Eddie Torres,
And feel the heat of Tito Puente.

Put on your dancing shoes,
To join them on the dancing floor,
They are the Salsa dancers.

Russian Kisses

Was it on Red Square
Or was it in St. Petersburg?
I cannot recall,
It's been so long ago.

The fire in her wide eyes
Enraptured my soul.
The luscious tone of her voice
Delighted my senses.

Her vibrant touch opened energy centers
Until then unknown.
And when she kissed,
It was with the passion of a revolutionary.

Daughter of the revolution or hidden royalty?
I'll never know.
Sweet Russian kisses,
DA!

Daughter of Heaven

You are so beautiful,
Your natural charm captivates the spirit,
I love you dearly,
O daughter of heaven.

The fluttering of your hair,
The sad look in your eyes
And your melancholic smile
Reveal the loneliness hidden in your heart.

Take me over the clouds
And sing me a lullaby
To appease my senses
And to ease the pain.

Your passionate kisses
And the way you make love
Arouse deep feelings
All over my being.

I've had moments of pleasure
But with you it's an ecstasy,
A soaring euphoria
That hits a crescendo.

You are so beautiful
Your natural charm captivates the spirit
I love you dearly
O daughter of heaven

A Whisper in the Wind

I search for you,
in the dark alleys,
I can't find you.

I search for you,
on the street corners,
I can't find you

I search for you,
in the hourly rate motels,
I can't find you.

In despair I call your name,
to tell you, "I still love you."
All I got in return is a whisper in the wind.

A Glimpse of You

What wouldn't I give for a glimpse of you?
What wouldn't I give for holding you in my arms?
What wouldn't I give for looking at you in the eyes?
And say, I love you!

What wouldn't I give for a glimpse of you?
But you belong to someone else
And I will never have you.
What wouldn't I give for a glimpse of you?

The Lost Flower

I went to sleep
And I had a dream.
I dreamt that I was in heaven.
I picked up the prettiest flower
I had ever seen.
I woke up from my dream,
To find the flower in my hand.
I was delighted.
But the gods are mischievous.
In order for me to keep the flower,
I had to forgo my dream.
The clock was ticking,
I hesitated...
I lost the flower and
I couldn't go back to my dream.

Wounds of Illusion

Three times, the leaves
Have changed colors,
And my feelings for you
Have remained constant.
I catered to your mind,
And not reaching your heart,
Only to learn too late that
Life cannot go on
Without touching the heart.
Why didn't I bring you more flowers?
Why didn't we have more to share?
Now that you are gone,
I can feel the pain,
The pain of losing you.
And my wounded heart wonders,
Wonders whether the wounds
Are wounds of illusion?

Lost Love

The love between us
vanished like a dream.
I've suffered enough.
Please, let me go.

I want to embark
On a new journey
to a lofty stratum
into the unknown.

Awaiting me there
is an ecstasy
never before enjoyed
by a mortal soul.

Now is the time
to bid you farewell.
I can't be with you
our love died out.

The Lady of the Garden

Once there was a man who was unhappy with his life;
He consulted a wise man who told him:
"Leave your city on the new moon and walk straight for two days,
You will find a magical city where happiness abounds."

On the day of the new moon he left and traveled until night.
He came upon a garden tendered by a witty young lady.
They had dinner together while watching the stars.
Charmed by her soothing voice he invited her
to the magical city.

The lady declined saying that as the Lady of the Garden
She was forever bound to the land and could not leave.
Disappointed and tired the man decided to go to sleep.
He placed his shoes facing the direction he was traveling.

While he slept, the wise man that was following him
Turned the shoes around in the direction he came from.
At the dawn of the day the man got up and put his shoes on.
He traveled for a whole day until the night came down.

He found a city that looked like the one he had left behind;
However the people in this new city were so happy and nice.
They showered him with love and affection.
He decided to stay there and he lived happily ever after.

The Pursuit of Happiness

Whoever said: "life is the pursuit of Happiness,"
has never experienced the human heart's trickiness.
To pursue happiness is to be bound for misery.
Only for a moment can life be a bowl of cherry.

How wonderful it was for us to be together!
How nice to have something good to remember.
But the dream is gone. It is time to move on.
All good things come to an end. I must carry on.

I began to think about the people who have been good to me.
Those who brought the sunshine in my life to a higher degree,
by a little kindness, an expression of love and a lot of patience.
I am thankful to you for chatting with me over long distance.

I don't know if our paths will cross again.
And if they do I hope we have nothing to explain.
Only that we come together in love and happiness
With an untarnished heart that knows no bitterness.

Boundless Abyss

I traveled to the end of the world looking for you.
I visited the boundless abyss searching for you
Never realizing all this time
That you were always here with me.

The Lady of Jamaica Estates

She was rich like a queen,
With no one to fulfill her dream.
All she wanted in her relationship
Was a second honeymoon on a cruise-ship.

Her husband couldn't fulfill her dreams.
He was always busy working.
He made promises after promises.
But he couldn't leave his businesses.

Finally he made a commitment,
To take an early retirement.
But on the wee morning hour,
He died while taking a shower.

She was rich like a queen,
With no one to fulfill her dream.
Enjoy what you have today,
Love cannot wait another day.

Hand in Hand
To President Obama

How soothing it is to recall
The time Grandma took me on a stroll.
Hand in hand we went down the street,
While the night lights were still lit.

The quiet "Hello" of a passerby,
Covered by the bells of a church nearby.
The whispering of an "I love you,"
The sun's reflection in the morning dew.

A dog walking over to sniff my face,
A pat on the head, a long embrace.
Signs of affection between old friends,
Who may never see each other again.

Grandma was always watching
With protective feeling.
She is now watching me in the divine light.
You see, Grandma passed away last night.

Matilda
To my English teacher

I was fascinated by the long black dreadlocks
that fell so graciously on her back,
touching a yellow ribbon tight around her waist.
Gold earrings, in her pierced ears,
enlivened her lovely white dress.
A gold chain hung around her neck.
The whole ensemble of white, yellow and gold
matched her beautiful black face, as she said loudly:
"Mammy, Mammy can I have a coloring book,."
"No, Matilda," said the mother.
Matilda didn't take no for an answer, she started to pout,
causing the small gold chain to wave about her neck.
"Mammy, I could use it for my book report," she pleaded,
looking at her mother with her large brown eyes.
Mother couldn't resist such a convincing argument.
"You can have a coloring book,"
she told Matilda.
Matilda made a fast run for the bookshelves.
Like a ballerina she stood on the tips of her white shoes,
showing the yellow stripes on her white socks,
that matched flawlessly with the rest of her outfit.
She extended her right arm
and grabbed two books with her little hand
that seemed to exert a Herculean force.

She turned to her mother with a lovely smile,
revealing a set of white teeth shining over violet gums.
Her large nose shrank as her little cheeks expanded.
"I said only one book." the mother yelled.
Matilda's lovely smile disappeared,
A disappointing frown covered Matilda's sad face.
Then, a shopper walked up to the mother and said,
"Here is a coupon; you can use it for your purchase."
She took the coupon and said "Oh, thank you!"
The little girl got her two books.
She left the bookstore jumping happily
And then disappeared into the crowd.
I can still remember her lovely silhouette
and those long black dreadlocks
that floated on her white and yellow dress.

A New York Minute

Everything can change
in a New York Minute.
That's the lesson we drew from 9/11.
Life is so ephemeral,
one minute we're here,
the next minute...
we're gone forever.
Two things remain however,
it's the good deeds we've done
for our fellow human beings
And the eternal "I love you."

Love on-line

With a little box in our hands,
We connect with the whole world.
Web browsing is a cinch,
But how do we connect with ourselves?

All we need to do is to close our eyes
And open up our heart and soul.
We will discover a sacred place,
That holds past, present and future.

In the magical stillness of it all,
A great truth shall be revealed to us:
Love permeates the whole universe,
And love is what keeps us going.

Part Three:
Nature

Autumn's Leaves
To Meredith

Nature is entering its resting phase.
Leaves are changing colors,
Giving off their very best,
for the enjoyment of the appreciative traveler.

The leaves will not be seen again.
The wind carries them into oblivion,
dressed in bright costumes,
like soldiers saluting Caesar before a mortal combat.

These were my thoughts as she passed by me.
Then a ray of sunshine shone over her golden hair,
laid freely over her back,
in a lovely display of natural simplicity.

She was totally unaware of the beauty she radiated
and the affectionate feelings she inspired,
as much as the leaves were unaware of their splendor
and the wonderful joy they bring to us.

"You have the most beautiful hair I've ever seen", I told her.
She became embarrassed and still she said, "Thank you."
Then she disappeared into nothingness,
Carried away by the wind, like the autumn's leaves.

Midnight Dream

She comes into the night as sweet as a dove,
A ball of fire that ignites an explosion of love.
Hidden in her bosom is a cornucopia of joy,
A fleeting fantasy, a beautiful dream to enjoy.

Slowly she opens up to expose her nudity,
Revealing in the dark her esoteric body,
An intricate web of beads and filaments,
That will only last for short moments.

She embraces the unknown in a passionate move,
Moaning sounds of pleasure for being in the groove.
Deep and powerful, she penetrates the night,
With distinctive flagrance and exquisite delight.

The erection is gone, calm returns to nature.
The flower folds its petals, calling for closure.
I refresh with droplets flowing from a stream.
At the stroke of midnight, am I having a dream?

Powderhouse In the Morning

As I start my morning stretch,
I look through the window.
On the other side of the valley,
The mountain is covered with snow.

I can see the narrow road
That divides the field in two parts.
Closer to me is the village's church
Raising its steeple in the sky.

Over in the distance,
A cow is grazing in the field.
All is quiet; I continued my morning stretch,
It's Powderhouse in the morning

Noxontown

In the wilderness of the Florida Everglades,
A flower salutes the morning sun with vitality.
Up, up in the sky a glider defies the law of gravity,
In man's eternal search to reach for the stars.

Under the watchful eyes of God's creature
And in harmony with the best in nature,
I pause for one brief shining moment,
To reflect on the serenity of the environment.

The journey ended as the night came down.
Will I ever forget my friends of Noxontown?
Having gathered my moss I return to my roots.
For love is awaiting me in a place called home.

Bird's Nest

Do birds have memory?
or is there an encoded message in their brain,
that tells them everything they need to know,
in order to start a new family?

Year after year in springtime,
a hard-working bird would build up a nest
behind my front porch lantern,
following a tradition that started a long time ago.

She was so busy all day long with her partner,
transporting small branches to build the nest.
The next days she continued to work,
until the nest was to her satisfaction.

A marvel of architecture,
a piece of art with interwoven branches.
It had to be nice indeed,
that's where the children will be born.

She had so much love in her heart,
no matter how many times she was disturbed,
she would rest for a moment on the power line
and always come back to prepare for her family.

A Morning Concert
To Jessica

It's the beginning of spring,
Four thirty every morning,
On top of my cherry tree, birds get together,
To salute the morning and sing to each other.

I can't stand the noise.
I am losing my poise.
All I want in my very small way,
Is only to sleep tight until day.

How can I sleep, when perched on their tower,
Facing my window at such an early hour,
Birds are filling the air with a morning concert,
With no concern for my personal request.

"There must be something wrong,
In wanting to silence any song.,"
Wrote Robert Frost the poet.
There is also a time to be quiet.

Reference: Robert Frost, "A Minor Bird"

A Bird's Song
In Memory of MLK

I hear a bird singing.
It's a cry from the heart
That unites all the birds
From mountains to valley.

I hear a bird singing.
It's a song of freedom
That sweeps all over
This great land of ours.

I hear a bird singing.
But on a balcony
In Memphis, Tennessee,
A bullet stops the song.

I hear a bird singing.
The bird is dead
But the song lives on
For other birds to sing.

Good-Bye

Good-bye sweet home.
I never thought I would leave you so soon,
And in my heart the feelings start to grow.
May the passing of the seasons teach me to let go.

I will remember your beauty in spring hours:
The multiple colors of your splendid flowers,
The friendly creatures that your environment nurtures
In the garden and pond by some miracle of nature,

Summer will bring back the sweet memories
Of moments shared with friends under cherry trees,
The sight and sound of children playing with water,
A bird walking on the lawn in clement weather.

Raking leaves in the fall was a family ritual,
Working together while singing a spiritual,
And the wind blowing leaves in my face
As it cleared the land's surface.

Winter under your roof was most enjoyable;
Leaving footprints in the snow is not always bearable.
I wish I could write your name on the walls of Time.
Your memory is engraved in my heart like a shrine.

Central Park

There is a spot in Central Park,
Where the road to happiness starts.
There, you'll find a new state of mind,
The natural settings to unwind.

Sharing your lunch with a squirrel
With a feeling of doing well.
Looking at joggers run,
In the heat of the mid-day's sun.

The cell phone is off to postpone a call.
Preferring the sounds of the waterfall.
On that spot in Central Park,
I let go like a butterfly and I feel on track.

A Smile

You can travel in the limelight
and be seen by all the people.
You can't accomplish an epic journey
If you are unkind to fellow travelers.

The essence of life is in a smile.
The more you give it away
The more it comes back to you.
Smile now, you'll get it back!

The Homeless Lady

In the New York City subway, a homeless lady,
On a wheel chair was passing the cup one evening.
Most commuters were dozing off;
Others did not want to be bothered.

One person however dropped a dollar bill
In the homeless lady's paper cup.
"Thank you," said the homeless lady, as she moved on.
Then she noticed the sad face of a tired little girl.

"Why are you so sad?" she asked the little girl,
Who was quite surprised but didn't utter a word.
"Give me a smile, I can't see you so sad," the lady said.
The little girl gave a blank face instead of a smile.

"Here, take the dollar and let me see you smile."
The little girl looked at her mother, who acquiesced.
She then accepted the dollar with a radiant smile.
The homeless lady left the train beaming with joy.

The Children of Dr. Grant

By the dozens they come to see him and his staff,
the lovely children of Dr. Grant.
You should see them playing in the hallway
or just laying down quietly in their strollers.

This one common thread unites them all,
the lovely children of Dr. Grant.
It's not the color of their skin,
spoken languages nor social status.

They all suffer from neuromuscular diseases,
the lovely children of Dr. Grant.
Some are confined to wheelchair since birth
and will carry this burden all their lives.

They receive the best known treatments,
the lovely children of Dr. Grant.
But this terrible disease is not fair,
to attack these innocent little ones.

The Evening Star

She was the prettiest
And also the brightest.
She could write poetry;
She understood people.

She was a passionate and compassionate lady
Who devoted her life to improving the lot
Of her nation's less fortunate children.
She was destined to do good for humanity.

She was a TV personality on her way to stardom.
One day she disappeared and never came back.
The killer breast cancer hit her, so they say.
The angels came down to carry her into heaven.

Sometimes I think of her, but as you can see,
In the dark of the night a star looks brighter.
As I lift up my eyes towards the constellations,
I realized that she was there as an evening star.

Boat People

From distant China to a nearby Caribbean nation,
People are heading towards a common destination.
It's called America, land of opportunity,
Freedom and beauty.

Unlike the African slaves who came because they were sold,
And Europeans who thought the streets were paved with gold,
These new comers risk their lives facing the impossible,
To come to America where dreams are still possible.

But the sea is not kind to travelers, it seems.
Many will never see the land of their dreams.
Their cold bodies will feed the marine creatures
Paying passage for such daring adventures.

Some of those who make it safely to these shores,
Will experience sufferings unknown to whores.
In the end, they will ask with sorrow in the heart:
"Why didn't I stay home and do my part?"

Dreaming in the Sun

I like to dream in the sun
By the blue sea,
Sharing the happiness
Of seagulls in the sky.

I Will Survive

Winter has taken over the beautiful flowers
They are now buried under snow showers.
Spring will return, winter doesn't last forever,
And the flowers will be prettier than ever.

A Bright Morning Star

Rejoice my fellow traveler.
You are approaching the city of God.
It is lit up by a bright morning star.
The sign says:
"At early dawn God will come to your aid".

PART FOUR:
Short Stories

The Goddess of the Waterfall

One night, when Dr. Hum was in a very good humor, Greg went to him and said:
"Please, Dr. Hum, can you tuck me in and tell me a story."
Dr. Hum cleared his throat with his usual sounds "hum, hum." And after pulling the comforter on Greg, he sat by his
bedside and told him the story of the Goddess of the Waterfall.

"After years of absence," Dr. Hum said, "I returned to the birthplace, to see the land and to visit with relatives. Two barking dogs met me at the house gate, followed by greetings from relatives.
First, I stopped at my ancestors' mausoleum for a little prayer. Then
I chatted over drinks with the relatives.
As the evening approached, I went under the orange tree that held so much memory. That's where I used to sit down and dream as a kid.
I can still remember one particular afternoon, when specially touched by the beauty of the scenery and enraptured by the distinctive aroma of the orange tree's white blossoms. I watched the sun go down slowly over the other side of the mountain, creating the most beautiful sunset I had ever experienced. The blue sky was transformed into a kaleidoscope of beautiful bright colors. Switching from blue to red and to purple, while the

sun changed from white gold to deep orange. Up on the hills, on the other side of the valleys, grazing cows, goats and sheep took part in this celebration of lights and colors, by displaying ribbons tied around their necks, horns and tails, while exotic birds were flying above them.

As the sun disappeared, the moon took over the sky and I followed its path at the foot of the mountain, near the big rock under which water of the village's brook came from. This was a sacred area full of mysticism.

That's where the Goddess of the Waterfall lived, in all the secrecy that was hidden under this mountain full of magic and mystery.

The Goddess was a young maiden of angelic beauty, with long black hair. She would sit on the rock, when nobody was around, to comb her hair with a magical gold comb. It was widely believed that anyone who found her comb would have great power and be immensely rich, but no one that I know of ever did. The Goddess was very careful not to leave her comb on the rock."

"Did the Goddess have any children?" Greg asked.

"No children," said Dr. Hum.

"The Goddess of the Waterfall did not have any children.

She wanted very much to have a little one to cherish. It was feared that she would steal any unattended child to take with her under the mountain where she lived, and this child would be deprived of mother and father. For this reason, children were never allowed to stay by the water without adult supervision.

Over all the years that the Goddess of the Waterfall lived in the village, very few people had seen her. That's why I was very intrigued when one day my cousin told me that she saw the Goddess of the Waterfall.

She explained to me that it was on a night when the moon was full and the valley was clear as on a bright sunny day. She hid behind a tree and waited very late, with goose bumps all over her body, to watch the
Goddess come out, swimming from under the waterfall.
The Goddess sat on the rock and started to comb her hair softly. As she turned for one moment, my cousin couldn't help but notice the melancholy on her beautiful face, probably due to the loneliness of living by herself under this big mountain without a companion.
This is why, every year on the first weekend of May, the people of the village would congregate by the waterfall, to put on a big celebration. This was to express their gratitude to the Goddess, for providing water and abundant crops. Relatives would come from afar to participate. Those who couldn't attend would send their contributions.
It was the only time during the year that people of the village were allowed to go under the waterfall, inside the mountain where the Goddess lived. My friends, who have been there, assured me that it was very beautiful, with paintings on the walls.
Visitors were only allowed into one room that was furnished with rocks, well arranged for people to sit down and enjoy the coolness under the mountain. The quarters of the Goddess were definitely off limits, although many people would have loved to see them.
The people of the village hoped that the Goddess would appear to them in person during this time of great celebration in her honor. But the
Goddess always found her own way to make her presence felt, as you will see in a moment.

The annual celebration would go on for three days, starting on Friday morning to end on Sunday evening. There was strict observance of rituals in the selection of songs and dances and the service of food and drinks.

I specially remember the so-called "Dinner of the Angels," which was given in honor of the Goddess, with the participation of the village's children.

It was set like a Viennese table and included all kinds of sweets generally enjoyed by children: assorted cakes and cookies, canolies, cassava, bread and rice pudding ceremoniously arranged on a linen tablecloth, under a tent by the waterfall. It was left there unattended on Saturday night, to give a chance to the Goddess to partake in it. No one was allowed to touch it during that time. Everybody knew that the Goddess had to be served first.

A cat was seen, moving around the table, in the middle of the night. The people rejoiced in the belief that the Goddess had used her magical power to transform herself into a cat to partake in this celebration in her honor.

On Sunday afternoon, after the waiting time had elapsed, the children would gather together around the table to sing the appropriate praising songs to the Goddess, one of which I still remember. It goes like this:

> *"O Beautiful Goddess of the water,*
> *This song was specially made for you.*
> *It's my way of telling you: 'I love you!'*
> *O beautiful Goddess of the water.*

> *"You are the most beautiful Goddess*
> *That ever lived in this whole valley.*

From my heart let me say: 'I love you!'
O beautiful Goddess of the water.

The music was led by a violinist, who would make the violin cry into the most angelic sounds of music ever heard by human ears. Some say that over the years, he had captured the soul of departed children that he kept inside the violin; that's why the music was so heavenly.
Then the food would be served, starting with the children, then the adults, and the music, songs and dances would continue well into the evening, with the violinist playing relentlessly like a fiddler. On that Sunday evening, the celebration would end and everybody would return home fully recharged to face the obligations of daily living."
Greg said to Dr. Hum, "What happened to the Goddess?"
Dr. Hum looked down for a moment, took a deep breath then said:
"A bad king came into power, darkness covered the land. The children left the village. Services to the Goddess stopped. No one saw her combing her hair on the big rock anymore."
Dr. Hum concluded that the Goddess had a broken heart.
Then one day, the violinist decided to rekindle an old flame. He took his violin with him along with a dose of courage, and went under the waterfall, inside the mountain, searching for the Goddess that he loved so much. As he sat on a rock bench playing wonderful praising songs, the
Goddess appeared in a misty blue dress and sat near him.
Charmed by her deep eyes, he continued to play with all his heart.
The music never stopped. He's been playing for her ever since. And the song goes on:

> *"O beautiful Goddess of the water,*
> *This song was specially made for you.*
> *It's my way of telling you: 'I love you!*
> *O beautiful Goddess of the water."*

As Dr. Hum sang that song he noticed that Greg had fallen soundly asleep.

He pulled the cover over him, turned off the light and closed the door.

Then he stopped for one moment and went "Hum, hum."

Dr. Hum's Little Kitty
To Debbie, Edith, Kathay

Dr. Hum had a gray, fuzzy little kitty that he loved very much. His name was Kato.

One day Kato was taking a stroll, along with his mother and his two sisters. He stopped here and there to play, catching up in leaps with them. Then, somehow he got separated from his family.

When the mother realized that Kato was missing, she became frantic and started looking for him. Still she couldn't find him. A big search was arranged to look for Kato, with help from the neighborhood cats. Even a search dog volunteered his service, in trying to locate the poor missing little kitty.

They looked all over for Kato, under the trees and in the flower bushes.

It was already dark and they were still searching, using big flashlights with intense light. Kato had wandered into another direction and could not be found.

The search party realized that the missing kitten was not going to be located in the dark. The search was called off, to resume in the morning.

With sorrow in her heart the mother returned home, praying that Kato would find his way back home.

It was a cold, windy and snowy night. Poor little kitty was still wandering. He didn't know where he was heading. He didn't know what was going to happen to him. He felt so lonely, he was so afraid. He missed his family, even though he couldn't stand his baby sister Katrina who got all the attention from mother and everyone else. He wanted his Mom who would provide him with warm comfort and also some milk. He was so cold, hungry and afraid. Out of fear and desperation he started to cry. He wiped the teardrops from his eyes with his little paw. Kato continued to walk in the cold winter looking for a place to spend the night. Fortunately he found shelter under the hood of a car that was parked on the street, in front of a big house. Hungry and tired he curled himself up in between the engine and the car body, hoping that in the morning his mother would find him.

It was so cold he could hardly sleep. When he finally did get some sleep, he had a nightmare. He dreamt that he was playing with his two sisters and having a real good time, but a big dog came running after him trying to eat him alive.

He woke up suddenly upon hearing a thundering noise. It was the engine of the car that was turned on by the owner. The poor little kitty panicked and jumped on the ground in a hurry, screaming *"meow!, meow!"*

His cry attracted the driver's attention. Kato turned his head to look while fleeing. He couldn't believe his eyes. It was Dr. Hum. They were so happy to find each other.

Dr. Hum took Kato in his strong arms and held him to his heart with love and tenderness while expressing a feeling of joy and forgiveness.

It was like a scene that went straight to the heart, like in Rembrandt's painting, "The Return of the Prodigal Son."

True love has no limits. A big party was thrown in Kato's honor, to celebrate his return. All the neighborhood cats that participated in the search were invited and also the big search dog who made Kato very nervous.

Kato received many presents from family and friends who came to express their love for him. He was so touched, he rubbed his body against Dr. Hum's legs in sign of gratitude.

Dr. Hum looked at Kato and went: "Hum, hum."

After all, it turned out to be per-r-r-fect day!

Greg's Goldfish
To the Gedeons

In Greg's backyard lays an ornate pond, filled with goldfishes. They were given to him on his eleventh birthday. The goldfishes are self-reliant and easygoing, and Greg does not even have to feed them. They find their subsistence in the decomposed leaves and insects that get in the water from the nearby trees. Since the pond is circular, with a column at its center, the fishes go around and around, playing endlessly all the time.

One particular hot summer day, Greg noticed that some of the fishes were heading toward the surface of the water gasping for air. Greg called Dr. Hum and asked him for his advice. Dr. Hum started by clearing his throat in his usual way by emitting the sound "hum, hum", then he indicated that at the higher temperature less gas was getting dissolved in the water, making it harder for the fishes to get the proper amount of oxygen needed to survive. Then, with his help, Greg placed the fishes in buckets of fresh water and transferred them to his friend Joe's aquarium, leaving the pond in its natural state, somewhat muddy with decayed leaves.

Autumn went, followed by a harsh winter. Water in the pond turned into solid ice. A white sheet of snow covered the green grass. Nature fell into a deep sleep.

Then one day, when spring had returned and the ice in the pond had melted away, Greg was reading quietly by the pond, when, to his great surprise, he noticed fishes swimming in the water.

He rushed to the house to inform Dr. Hum of this amazing news.

"That's impossible, there can't be fishes in the pond!" Dr. Hum told Greg. He went outside to look, and there they were, a colony of small fishes cruising the water, going around and around and playing endlessly, like their ancestors had done before them. Dr. Hum was totally flabbergasted. To top it off, Greg looked at him in the eyes and said to him: "You see, Dr. Hum, you didn't trust me."

"I am sorry, my child," Dr. Hum replied with deep embarrassment.

He scratched his head for a logical explanation, only to be convinced that before signing off, the old generation of fishes had left enough eggs in the muddy sand to start a new life over. He told Greg that in this manner, the tradition of renewal, long ago established, will always continue.

"It is written," Dr. Hum said, "A fish's eyes never close."

Then, wanting to know more about goldfish, Greg said to him: "Dr. Hum, where did goldfish come from?"

Dr. Hum looked at Greg as if searching for an answer. Then he said,

"Why don't we sit down?"

They sat down on the bench by the fishpond.

And this is the story of the king's goldfish that he told:

The King's Goldfish
To Sara

"Hum, hum," began Dr. Hum.

A long, long time ago there was a young king named Tang who ruled over the great land of China. He was always in a grouchy mood and he stayed in his room most of the time, complaining of weakness. His doctors could not find anything physically wrong with him.

This was a matter of grave concern for his advisors, who didn't know what to do. They called upon the wise men of the land who deliberated for many weeks before they finally came to the conclusion that what the young king needed was a pet to keep him company. Messengers were sent over the whole land to announce that whomever would bring a pet that was pleasing to the king would be greatly rewarded.

On the day of the presentation people came with some very interesting pets. There were all kinds of animals big and small. Some of them, the king had already seen. Others were a curiosity to him and to his court.

Noticing that the king did not show any interest in the selection of the animals as pets, the wise men picked 12 of them for him to choose from. They were rat, ox, tiger, rabbit, dragon, boar, dog, snake, cock, monkey, sheep and horse. But to the disappointment of the wise men, the king did not accept any of them. The wise men decided then to use these animals to form the Chinese zodiac. They thought that all hope was lost in trying to find a pet for the king.

But, as the presentation was coming to an end, a young lady walked in, carrying a bowl covered with a piece of cloth bearing the design of a fish on it. Her beautiful face indicated that she was tired. Indeed she had traveled a long way, having come from a distant village.

At first she was refused entrance to the palace. But she insisted on her right to make her presentation to the king. She was laughed at. But she didn't pay any attention to the people who made fun of her. She didn't reveal to anyone what she carried with her. She was very resolved to see the king.

When she finally arrived in front of the king, she placed the bowl of water in front of him and bowed her head in salute.

The young king admired her youthful beauty and told her: "Please show me what you have." She lifted the cloth with the fish design that covered the bowl. The king looked in the clear water and saw two beautiful goldfishes swimming and playing to their hearts' content. He had never seen such beautiful little fishes before. Joy overtook him and he regained his health at once. And it was all because he had finally found the pet that was pleasing to him.

He ordered a fishpond to be built in the palace garden for the goldfishes, so he could watch them as they played in the water. He was so happy that he took the hand of the young lady as his bride.

Poetry and stories were written about how the goldfish brought back strength and happiness to the king. In the folklore of the land, the gold- fish became the symbol of courage and virility for male children and good luck for little girls.

The king had many children with his young wife and his dynasty lasted for centuries.

From China, the goldfish was introduced to Japan and to the countries of Europe, such as Italy, France, and England. Catherine the Great of
Russia admired the goldfish for its great beauty.
The goldfish found its way to the United States from Europe.

When the story ended, Greg sat quietly for a moment. Then he said to Dr. Hum: "Where do they sell goldfish?"
"At most pet shops," answered Dr. Hum.
"I'll tell all my friends," Greg said.
Dr. Hum smiled and cleared his throat in his usual way, "Hum, Hum."

The Rabbi's Gift

Before I go to bed at night, I like to read a story from one of the
"Chicken Soup for the Soul" books. There is one particular story that keeps me pondering on its profound message for all of us. It's called "The Rabbi's gift."
I urge you to read the original version in "Chicken Soup for the Soul", book one, by Mark Victor Hansen and Jack Canfield, I promise, you will be enlightened. In the meantime, let me tell you the story in my own words, as I recall it from memory.
There were five monks who lived in an old monastery by themselves without any followers. The young people had stopped joining the priesthood and the parishioners were not interested in the teachings of the monks. The five monks were at a lost in trying to rebuild their congregation.
They had many brainstorming sessions in addition to prayers and fasting but that did not help. No one showed up not even for Sunday mass.
Out of desperation the father superior, father Abbott, decided to pay a visit to the rabbi who lived not far from them, hoping that in his infinite wisdom the rabbi would come up with a solution for their problem.
The rabbi received him joyfully. He offered him tea and crackers and they had a long conversation and a prayer session. But at the end, father Abbott realized that the rabbi did not have an advice for him as to how to revive his congregation.

The rabbi told him he was sorry, and as he bid him farewell he said to father Abbott,
"Take a look at the fourth Gospel, among you stands the one you do not know."
Father Abbott returned to the dying monastery and reported on the failure of his mission to the other four monks. As he concluded his report, father Abbott told the monks that he was very puzzled by the last words of the rabbi. "What did he say?" one of them asked,
"He said to read the fourth Gospel, among you stands the one you do not know" father Abbott answered.
The monks became silent as they reflected on the meaning of the last words of the rabbi. "Among you stands the one you do not know."
They all hit their bible and started to read the fourth Gospel. Sure enough the words of the rabbi were there,

"Among you stands the one you do not know"
$\qquad\qquad\qquad\qquad$ **-John 1:26**

"Among us," They thought.
Who would that be?
Each one was thinking, was it father Abbott, brother Thomas, brother Elred, brother Phillip or was it me?
Since each one of the monks could not be sure as to which one of them was the leader, to be on the safe side, they began to treat each other with high respect and admiration.
This new attitude did not escape the vigilant eyes of the people of the village who noticed the glow on the face of the monks and the reverence with which they treated one another. People began to seek spiritual advice from the transformed monks.

Young people were asking to be admitted to sacerdotal services. Before long the congregation regained its membership.

A new wave of love and understanding swept over the whole village as people started to show high respect for one another. It was really wonderful.

And all this came to pass because of the Rabbi's gift.

Rejoice my fellow traveler.
You are approaching the city of God.
It is lit up by a bright morning star.
The sign says:
"At early dawn God will come to your aid".

ALPHABETIZED INDEX

A Bird's Song 74
A Bright Morning Star 84
A Brighter World 6
A Cry in the Night 43
A Glimpse of You 53
A Little Place in the Sun 23
A Magic Thought 10
A Morning Concert 73
A New York Minute 64
A Smile 77
A Whisper in The Wind 52
Autumn's Leaves 68
Bird's Nest 72
Boat People 81
Boundless Abyss 59
Breakfast at Bruce's Bakery 25
Caught in the Thicket 7
Central Park 76
Chasing Clouds 16
Chrysalis 45
Dancing in the Park 19
Daughter of Heaven 50
Dialing God 4

Dreaming in the Sun 82
Embracing the Divine 41
First Love 36
First Step 26
Free 18
Greg's Goldfish 97
Gone with the Wind 24
Good-Bye 75
Hand in Hand 61
I Will Survive 83
I Wish 37
Let It Be Easy 5
Lost Love 56
Love On-Line 65
Matilda 62
Midnight Bloom 69
Nickie 38
Nolan 27
Noxontown 71
One More Time 32
Peace and Tranquility 22
Powderhouse in the Morning 70
Present Moment 13
Responsibility 31
Russian Kisses 49
Salsa Dancers 48
Spectrum of Beauty 47
Thanks 28
The Children of Dr. Grant 79
The Evening Star 80
The Gift 8

The Heart of the Lotus 30
The Homeless Lady 78
The King's Goldfish 99
The Lady of the garden 57
The Lady of Jamaica Estates 60
The Light 21
The Lonely Butterfly 46
The Long Journey 12
The lost Flower 54
The Point of Life 17
The Power of Forgiveness 11
The Pursuit of Happiness 58
The Secret 14
The Space between Us 42
True Wisdom 33
Tulip 15
Unconditional Love 39
Victory 29
What if... 9
When I am With You 44
Wounds of Illusion 55
You and I 40

ABOUT THE AUTHOR

Jesse Gourdet was born and raised in Haiti where he taught French literature for a few years.
He moved to the United States as a young adult and made his home in New York City.
He discovered his passion for the printed word while reading bedtime stories to his children.
He then started to write his own poems and short stories.
Jesse's poems have been published in the anthologies *The Colors of Life, Days Gone By, Time After Time, The Best Poems and Poets of 2004, The Rustling Leaves, The International Who's Who in Poetry.*
Jesse Gourdet lives with his wife, Yanick. They have a son and a daughter.
You can contact Jesse at Jgourdet@aol.com

www.ingramcontent.com/pod-product-compliance
Lightning Source LLC
Chambersburg PA
CBHW060328050426
42449CB00011B/2694